IT'S TIME TO EAT POTATOES

It's Time to Eat POTATOES

Walter the Educator

Silent King Books
A WhichHead Entertainment Imprint

Copyright © 2024 by Walter the Educator

All rights reserved. No part of this book may be reproduced in any manner whatsoever without written per- mission except in the case of brief quotations embodied in critical articles and reviews.

First Printing, 2024

Disclaimer

This book is a literary work; the story is not about specific persons, locations, situations, and/or circumstances unless mentioned in a historical context. Any resemblance to real persons, locations, situations, and/or circumstances is coincidental. This book is for entertainment and informational purposes only. The author and publisher offer this information without warranties expressed or implied. No matter the grounds, neither the author nor the publisher will be accountable for any losses, injuries, or other damages caused by the reader's use of this book. The use of this book acknowledges an understanding and acceptance of this disclaimer.

It's Time to Eat POTATOES is a collectible early learning book by Walter the Educator suitable for all ages belonging to Walter the Educator's Time to Eat Book Series. Collect more books at WaltertheEducator.com

USE THE EXTRA SPACE TO TAKE NOTES AND DOCUMENT YOUR MEMORIES

POTATOES

It's time to eat potatoes, round and so brown,

It's Time to Eat
Potatoes

Grown deep in the soil, hidden down.

From fields and gardens, they're dug with care,

Little earthy treasures waiting there.

Boiled or baked, they're soft and warm,

A cozy delight in every form.

With butter or salt, they taste so fine,

Potatoes make every meal shine!

In mashed potato bowls, fluffy and white,

They're creamy and smooth, a tasty sight.

With gravy or plain, a favorite treat,

A soft, warm bite that's hard to beat.

In crispy french fries, golden and long,

Potatoes sing a crunchy song.

Dipped in ketchup or eaten plain,

Each little fry is pure joy to gain.

It's Time to Eat
Potatoes

In soups, they float like tiny boats,

With carrots and peas, they bob and gloat.

Soft and tender, in each spoonful they lay,

Making soup cozy in every way.

In roasted chunks, they're brown and sweet,

With a crispy edge, they're fun to eat.

Sprinkled with herbs, so fragrant and nice,

Each little piece is a tasty slice.

In hash browns at breakfast, they sizzle and pop,

Golden and crunchy, they never stop.

With eggs or alone, they're a morning cheer,

Bringing warm flavors we hold dear.

Potatoes as chips, thin and round,

Crunching and munching, a crispy sound.

In bags or bowls, they make us smile,

It's Time to Eat
Potatoes

A salty snack that lasts a while.

Potato salad, cool and neat,

With veggies and dressing, it's fun to eat.

In picnics and lunches, it finds its place,

Adding a creamy, tasty grace.

So next time you see one, give a cheer,

For potatoes bring joy year after year.

From fields to our plates, they're hearty and true,

It's Time to Eat
Potatoes

A golden delight, just for you!

It's time to eat Potatoes, so yellow and bright,

ABOUT THE CREATOR

Walter the Educator is one of the pseudonyms for Walter Anderson. Formally educated in Chemistry, Business, and Education, he is an educator, an author, a diverse entrepreneur, and he is the son of a disabled war veteran. "Walter the Educator" shares his time between educating and creating. He holds interests and owns several creative projects that entertain, enlighten, enhance, and educate, hoping to inspire and motivate you. Follow, find new works, and stay up to date with Walter the Educator™ at WaltertheEducator.com

Milton Keynes UK
Ingram Content Group UK Ltd.
UKHW020047271124
451585UK00012B/1110